Grateful acknowledgment is made to the following for permission to reprint previously published material:

Addison-Wesley Publishing Company, Inc., for "Oodles of Noodles" from OODLES OF NOODLES by Lucia M. and James L. Hymes, Jr. Copyright © 1964 by Lucia M. and James L. Hymes, Jr. Reprinted by permission.

John Ciardi for "Someone's Face" from THE MAN WHO SANG THE SILLIES by John Ciardi. Copyright © 1961 by John Ciardi (Lippincott).

William Cole for "It's Such a Shock" by William Cole. Copyright © 1977 by William Cole.

Doubleday & Company, Inc., for "Song of the Pop-Bottlers" from A BOWL OF BISHOP by Morris Bishop. Copyright 1954 by Morris Bishop. Reprinted by permission of Doubleday & Company, Inc.

E. P. Dutton & Company, Inc., for "Wiggly Giggles" from ME IS HOW I FEEL: POEMS by Stacy Jo Crossen and Natalie Anne Covell. Copyright © 1970 by A. Harris Stone, Stacy Crossen, Natalie Covell, and Victoria deLarrea. A Saturday Review Press book. Reprinted by permission of E. P. Dutton, a division of New American Library.

Harper & Row, Publishers, Inc., for "Examination" from A LIGHT IN THE ATTIC: Poems and Drawings by Shel Silverstein. Copyright © 1981 by Snake Eye Music, Inc. Reprinted by permission of Harper & Row, Publishers, Inc. British rights administered by Jonathan Cape Ltd.

Bobbi Katz for "Doctor Croc." Copyright © 1985 by Bobbi Katz.

William Morrow & Company, Inc., for "Dora Diller" from THE NEW KID ON THE BLOCK by Jack Prelutsky. Copyright © 1984 by Jack Prelutsky. Reprinted by permission of Greenwillow Books, a Division of William Morrow & Company, Inc.

Alastair Reid for "Squishy Words" by Alastair Reid.

Russell & Volkening, Inc., as agents for the author, for "The Folk Who Live in Backward Town" from HELLO AND GOOD-BY by Mary Ann Hoberman. Copyright © 1959 by Mary Ann Hoberman. Published by Little, Brown & Company.

Karen S. Solomon for "Change in the Weather" by Ilo Orleans.

Library of Congress Cataloging-in-Publication Data: Main entry under title: A Popple in your pocket and other funny poems. SUMMARY: A collection of humorous verses by a variety of poets. 1. Children's poetry, American. 2. Humorous poetry, American. [1. American poetry—Collections. 2. Humorous poetry] I. Katz, Bobbi. II. Ewers, Joe, ill. PS586.3.P66 1986 811'.07'08 85-43342 ISBN: 0-394-88042-0

Manufactured in the United States of America 1 2 3 4 5 6 7 8 9 0

A Popple in Your Pocket and Other Funny Poems

Selected by Bobbi Katz

Illustrated by Joe Ewers

Random House 🏠 New York

Pop a Popple in Your Pocket

Pop a Popple in your pocket
And you never will be sad,
Because Popples make you giggle
And giggles make you glad!
With a Popple in your pocket
All your problems will be small,
And the things that make you worry
Will not worry you at all!

Do you feel a little nervous
When you're in the dentist's chair?
With a Popple in your pocket
You won't even care you're there!
Did your bike get a flat tire?
Did you miss your turn at bat?
With a Popple in your pocket
You will laugh at things like that!

Bobbi Katz

Wiggly Giggles

I've got the wiggly-wiggles today,
And I just can't sit still.
My teacher says she'll have to find
A stop-me-wiggle pill.

I've got the giggly-giggles today;
I couldn't tell you why.
But if Mary hiccups one more time
I'll giggle till I cry.

I've got to stamp my wiggles out
And hold my giggles in,
Cause wiggling makes me giggle
And gigglers never win.

Stacy Jo Crossen
and Natalie Anne Covell

I Eat My Peas with Honey

I eat my peas with honey;
I've done it all my life.
It makes the peas taste funny,
But it keeps them on the knife.

Anonymous

Oodles of Noodles

I love noodles. Give me oodles.
Make a mound up to the sun.
Noodles are my favorite foodles.
I eat noodles by the ton.

Lucia and James L. Hymes, Jr.

I Raised a Great Hullabaloo

I raised a great hullabaloo
When I found a large mouse in my stew.
Said the waiter, "Don't shout
And wave it about,
Or the rest will be wanting one, too!"

Anonymous

Dora Diller

"My stomach's full of butterflies!"
lamented Dora Diller.
Her mother sighed. "That's no surprise,
you ate a caterpillar!"

Jack Prelutsky

It's Such a Shock

It's such a shock, I almost screech,
When I find a worm inside my peach!
But then, what really makes me blue,
Is to find a worm who's bit in two!

William Cole

Through the Teeth

Through the teeth
And past the gums,
Look out, stomach,
Here it comes!

Anonymous

I Love You

I love you, I love you,
I love you divine,
Please give me your bubble gum,
You're *sitting* on mine!

Anonymous

Examination

from *A Light in the Attic*

I went to the doctor—
He reached down my throat,
He pulled out a shoe
And a little toy boat,
He pulled out a skate
And a bicycle seat,
And said, "Be more careful
About what you eat."

Shel Silverstein

Doctor Croc

My doctor is a crocodile
with a wily reptile smile.
I look at him and 1–2–3
the germs get scared
right out of me!

Bobbi Katz

Tongue Twisters

You've no need to light a night light
On a light night like tonight,
For a night light's light's a slight light,
And tonight's a night that's light.

When a night's light, like tonight's light,
It is really not quite right
To light night lights with their slight lights
On a light night like tonight.

Anonymous

The Tutor

A tutor who tuted the flute
Tried to tutor two tooters to toot.
Said the two to the tutor,
"Is it harder to toot or
to tutor two tooters to toot?"

Carolyn Wells

A Canner

A canner exceedingly canny
One morning remarked to his granny,
"A canner can can
Anything that he can,
But a canner can't can a can, can he?"

Anonymous

Song of the Pop-Bottlers

Pop bottles pop-bottles
In pop shops;
The pop-bottles Pop bottles
Poor Pop drops.

When Pop drops pop-bottles,
Pop-bottles plop!
Pop-bottle-tops topple!
Pop mops slop!

Stop! Pop'll drop bottle!
Stop, Pop, stop!
When Pop bottles pop-bottles,
Pop-bottles pop!

Morris Bishop

Did You Ever Go Fishing?

Did you ever go fishing on a bright sunny day—
Sit on a fence and have the fence give way?
Slide off the fence and rip your pants,
And see the little fishes do the hootchy-kootchy dance?

Anonymous

Toot! Toot!

A peanut sat on a railroad track,
His heart was all a-flutter;
The five-fifteen came rushing by—
Toot! toot! peanut butter!

Anonymous

Fatty, Fatty, Boom-a-latty

Fatty, Fatty, Boom-a-latty;
This is the way he goes!
He is so large around the waist,
He cannot see his toes!

This is Mr. Skinny Linny;
See his long lean face!
Instead of a regular suit of clothes,
He wears an umbrella case!

Anonymous

Ladles and Jellyspoons

Ladles and jellyspoons:
I come before you
To stand behind you
And tell you something
I know nothing about.

Next Thursday,
The day after Friday,
There'll be a ladies' meeting
For men only.

Wear your best clothes
If you haven't any,
And if you can come
Please stay home.

Admission is free,
You can pay at the door.
We'll give you a seat
So you can sit on the floor.

It makes no difference
Where you sit;
The kid in the gallery
Is sure to spit.

Anonymous

The Folk Who Live in Backward Town

The folk who live in Backward Town
Are inside out and upside down.
They wear their hats inside their heads
And go to sleep beneath their beds.
They only eat the apple peeling
And take their walks across the ceiling.

Mary Ann Hoberman

Change in the Weather

I think it would be very good
To have some snow and sleet
In summer when
We need it most
To drive away the heat.

Ilo Orleans

Squishy Words
(to be said when wet)

Squiff
Squidge
Squamous
Squinny
Squelch
Squash
Squeegee
Squirt
Squab

Alastair Reid

Someone's Face

Someone's face was all frowned shut,
All squeezed full of grims and crinkles,
Pouts and scowls and gloomers, but
I could see behind the wrinkles—
Even with her face a-twist,
I saw Someone peeking through.

And when Someone's nose was kissed,
Guess who came out giggling–YOU!

John Ciardi

Pop Goes a Popple

Up and down and all around
The Popples pep up people.
When people say, "I won't have fun!"
Pop goes a Popple!

A penny for a spool of thread,
A penny for a needle,
That's the way the money goes—
Pop goes a Popple!

Popples won't let people frown,
Scowl or sulk or worry.
When people say, "It can't be done!"
Pop goes a Popple!

Pretty Bit Popple